DON'T YOU JUST HATE THAT?

DON'T YOU JUST HATE THAT?

947
OF LIFE'S
LITTLE
ANNOYANCES

SCOTT COHEN

WORKMAN PUBLISHING · NEW YORK

Library of Congress Cataloging-in-Publication Data is available.
Library of Congress Control Number: 2020938523

ISBN 978-1-5235-0966-9

Design by Galen Smith

Workman books are available at special discounts when
purchased in bulk for premiums and sales promotions as
well as for fund-raising or educational use. Special editions
or book excerpts can also be created to specification. For
details, contact the Special Sales Director at the address
below, or send an email to specialmarkets@workman.com.

Workman Publishing Co., Inc.
225 Varick Street
New York, NY 10014-4381
workman.com

WORKMAN is a registered trademark of Workman Publishing Co., Inc.

Printed in the United States

First printing August 2020

10 9 8 7 6 5 4 3 2 1

Dedication

Have you ever had a friend who knows exactly what you do and do not need? In 2004, my friend Jeff set me up with Katie. He said she's perfect for me. I met her at a pub near her apartment in the West Village of Manhattan. A few weeks later, she told me she had moved to Portsmouth, New Hampshire. Her parents owned a bed and breakfast there—would I like to visit? Was she trying to drum up business for her Mom or were her thoughts more aligned with mine? I asked her where I would stay. She said there was an open room—she would get me the Friends and Family rate. Fearful of driving five hours to have Katie's mom hand me lighthouse and tubing pamphlets, I passed.

Three years later, Katie moved from Los Angeles to Brooklyn. While unpacking, she found a copy of the first edition of Don't You Just Hate That? *and decided to email me. I had included my email address at the end of the book in the slim possibility that I would meet someone. This new edition of* Don't You Just Hate That? *is dedicated to Katie, my wife, and our two boys, Tom and Neil, and to Jeff.*

Acknowledgments

When I submitted the final manuscript for *Don't You Just Hate That?* in 2004, I felt relieved to no longer need to catalog life's minor absurdities. Soon after the book was published, I sat at a restaurant bar waiting for a friend to arrive. A new *Don't You Just Hate That?* point came to me—I ignored it. But another came, and then another, and another. I reluctantly borrowed a pen from the bartender and scribbled the new points onto a cocktail napkin.

Fifteen years later, Danny Cooper, an editor at Workman Publishing, asked me if I had any new material. I told him I had written thousands of *Don't You Just Hate That?* points over the past fifteen years. We decided to rerelease the book, now updated to include hundreds of new annoyances. Thank you to Danny for reviving this book, and to Richard Rosen, the original editor— you both improved my material and made the process seamless and fun. A mentor of mine, another great editor, Tom Jenks, taught me that "Good is the enemy of great." I'm happy to have had the chance to improve this book—I hope you enjoy it.

DON'T YOU JUST HATE THAT?

1. When everything a cynic warns you about ends up happening.

2. Wondering if the appetizer you're sharing with a friend is being divided evenly.

3. Having to make that face to people in the hallway at work that implies, "Hey."

4. When someone with lame style compliments the outfit you're wearing.

5. When it takes scissors to open the plastic packaging containing scissors.

6. People who view karaoke as their chance to shine.

7. Kids who think "one more" means, "You can have another and then we'll argue about it from there."

8. Trading bad date stories with someone you're having a bad date with.

9. When you lose your phone and call it and end up speaking with some guy named Todd.

10. That the student who tells his classmates not to make it a popularity contest when voting for class president almost always loses the election.

11. Believing that a squirrel making direct eye contact with you is looking into your soul, when in fact it is trying to determine whether you have any nuts to share.

12. Being yelled at in a foreign language in a foreign country.

13.

14. Apartment buildings that don't have a 13th floor because of superstitious people.

15. When someone says, "I see you got a haircut," and makes no further comment.

16. Restaurants with indistinct figures, like a rooster and a chicken, indicating which restrooms are for men and women.

17. Watching a movie with your parents that shows full-frontal nudity.

18. Waiting behind people who look like they're in line but aren't.

19. What the "About the Author" on a book jacket doesn't tell you (e.g., "In addition, Scott has a man-crush on chef Gordon Ramsay.").

20. That it would be socially unacceptable, at your age, to wrap a Fruit Roll-Up around your pinky and suck on it for a few hours.

21. Finding a rusty AA battery, old packets of ketchup, and a picture of your aunt tossing a Frisbee as you search your glove compartment for your registration while the state trooper grows impatient.

22. That nailing a triple lutz in the Olympic figure skating finals is one of many joys you will never know.

23. When your nieces and nephews reach the age where they can distinguish a cheap gift from an expensive one.

24. That nursery school is just another forum for bullies.

25. That both Simon and Garfunkel went bald.

26. Having to preface the majority of what you say with, "I can't recall if I've mentioned this to you before, but . . ." because you're dating three people.

27. When your childhood friend who was always better than you at everything is still better than you at everything.

28. Feeling guilty for not socializing with the owners of the bed-and-breakfast where you're staying.

29. When a lady calls out, "Thanks a million!" and waves as her car pulls away, and you realize that you just gave her totally wrong directions.

30. An open parenthesis that is never closed (like this

31. The tiny percentage of times when song dedications played on the radio are actually heard by the person they're being dedicated to.

32. Wondering, having applied SPF 20 sunscreen, and then a layer of 40 an hour later, whether they average out to 30, they add up to 60, or it's only the last layer of 40 that counts.

33. When the most engaging human interaction of your day is answering, "Good," to the question, "How are you?"

34. Being unable to forget someone you spent twenty minutes with twenty years ago.

35. When someone knocks on plastic while saying, "Knock on wood."

36. The feeling you get when you clip your nail too far.

37. Having something valid to interject into the conversation of two nearby strangers but knowing that society does not permit you to do so.

38. That "I'm sure I'll see you around" really means, "Perhaps we'll bump into each other by accident."

39. Yoga instructors who smoke.

40. Taking notes not because there's any value to what's being said but because everyone else is taking notes.

41. Hating the fact that you say, "Muah!" whenever you kiss someone hello.

42. When you walk faster because the person in front of you looks attractive, and as you get a closer look you wish you hadn't bothered.

43. That you need to sing the alphabet in your head in order to figure out which letter comes after *W*.

44. People who ask the waiter absurd questions (e.g., "Was the lamb bottle-fed?").

45. That by the time most people have saved enough money to travel the world, they are too old to enjoy such a trip.

46. Recalling the tactless thing you said at the wake.

47. That bands named after a country or continent are usually lame (e.g., America, Europe, and Asia).

48. When your thigh rubs against a leather chair, emitting a loud, ripping noise, and every time you rub your leg against it again in an attempt to make the same noise to prove to the public that it wasn't a fart, it sounds nothing like the initial noise.

49. When your friend doesn't realize that you're trying to remove him from your life.

50. Parents who refuse to believe the negative things teachers say about their children at parent-teacher conferences.

51. When the driver pushes the unlock button as you pull the handle at the same moment.

52. When a party is too small to leave unnoticed.

53. Not being malicious enough to want your exes to live unhappily, but not being bighearted enough to want them to live a life free of regret.

54. When snowstorm sex turns to blackout sex.

55. Being unsure if someone is wearing a Halloween costume.

56. When you've waited so long to send a gift that sending one now would be more offensive than not.

57. When a game show contestant finishes with a negative score, and the host tries to cheer her up by saying, "Whelp, we enjoyed having you on the show!"

58. That the friends you spend the most time with aren't your favorite friends.

59. Street names that make you want to go on vacation (e.g., Ocean Breeze Road).

60. Walking by the same person you've already walked by in the dairy, produce, and frozen-food sections.

61. Feeling like another version of you took over when you were drunk and didn't do a very good job.

62. When a stranger shares a piece of extraneous information with you (e.g., "I see you're using a Mac. My cousin Jeff has a Mac.").

63. The moment you realize that "braving the hurricane" wasn't such a wise idea.

64. Wondering how strictly to adhere to the expiration date of a food item.

65. Missing fantasizing about what it would be like to be with the person you're now with.

66. People who say, "Pfssssst," while lifting weights.

67. Pretending to write down a confirmation number.

68. That we describe families as "nuclear."

Five Annoying Things About Being a Woman Working in a Men's Maximum-Security Prison

—*by A. L.*

1. That Kevin was offered three packs of cigarettes by another inmate if he would introduce me to him.

2. That a prison is full of men who notice when you get a haircut.

PROFESSIONALLY ANNOYED

3. When, as part of a pre-parole career preparation course, I had the class complete sample job applications, and one student asked, regarding the conviction question, "How do you spell 'hijack'?"

4. When your most well-received class, Grammar in the Slammer, is discontinued for bureaucratic reasons.

5. When an inmate tells me, "Aw, you don't need a boyfriend. You've got 2,300 boyfriends right here."

69. When the brief thrill of making the yellow light ends and you're bored again.

70. When you awake feeling fresh and ready to start the day and realize it's 3:17 a.m.

71. Nodding at the street performer to indicate, "You're far more talented and entertaining than I am, and I'm still not giving you a dollar."

72. TABLE 5:

Mr. & Mrs. John Randall
Mr. & Mrs. Dan Loew
Mr. & Mrs. David Chitwood
Mr. & Mrs. Kevin Walter
Deidre

73. Jogging with a friend who keeps a faster pace.

74. That the song "Take This Job and Shove It" failed to show the many hardships that the fellow endured later in life.

75. Remembering just enough French from high school to know that the two French people sitting across from you are talking about you.

76. Hearing a toilet flush on the other end of the phone.

77. When a friend says, "I have good news for you!" and it concerns her, not you.

78. When the person you're waving hello to doesn't see you waving, but then catches you awkwardly retracting the wave.

79. Feeling that you might fall through every time you step on a metal grate, despite the enormous likelihood that you won't.

80. Being the last person in a long line that no one else seems to be getting in.

81. The slow, insidious way that your love for something dies when you do it for a living.

82. People who drop cigarette butts on the sidewalk as if there are acceptable forms of littering.

83. Trying to collect unemployment along with 35 million other Americans.

84. Finding an old "To Do" list, most of which remains undone.

85. Sitting in a chair that is shorter than everyone else's.

86. A repetitious slog of boredom, isolation, anxiety, and despair. In other words, quarantining during a pandemic.

87. People who wear a tennis outfit to watch a tennis match.

88. Knowing more about the dermal papilla at the base of hair follicles than how to lead a happy life.

89. The frenzy that ensues when a cashier calls out, "This register is now open."

90. Towns that try to attract visitors by creating some idiotic, annual, record-breaking event.

91. Making out with someone who smells like airplane.

92. Male gynecologists.

93. When you're at a Greek restaurant and you want to order the lahanodolmades and the closest you can come to pronouncing it is to point at the menu and say, "That thing. Yeah that."

94. When stapling stapled staples jams your stapler with a staple.

95. When seeing men who are less attractive than you dating women who are more attractive than the women you date leads you to wonder if there's something wrong with your personality.

96. When your house is inadvertently listed on a star map as Justin Bieber's.

97. When you warmly thank the cashier for packing your groceries, but your attempt at brightening her day elicits no discernible reaction.

98. Bagel places that bomb you with cream cheese.

99. That the only place you seem to meet single people is your psychiatrist's waiting area.

100. That you expected the one hundredth point to be somehow more entertaining than the others.

101. *"Please speak your answers. For questions abou—"* "Customer service." *"Okay. I need to ask you a few questions first."*

102. That your teenage child is more sexually active than you.

103. That every generation thinks they have it the hardest.

104. When your dad sings the chorus of "Penny Lane" as "And Elaine . . ."

105. Having an urge while at work to tear your shoes and socks off and rub your finger between your sweaty toes, creating damp lint balls.

106. Textbooks depicting white Americans kindly trading with indigenous peoples, instead of, say, the Indian Removal Act by which 15,000 Cherokee were taken from their ancestral homelands.

107. When you're petting a dog and a stranger joins in, making you feel like you're involved in some sort of bizarre three-way.

108. When you can't stop thinking about a random, cryptic sign you saw (e.g., ASK ABOUT THE TREE TEA EXPERIENCE.).

109. The last razor-thin line of dirt that you can never quite get into the dustpan.

110. Pop-up ads that offer the removal of pop-up ads.

111. Having one of those days when your posts receive very few likes, causing you to feel alone in the world.

112. When the people in your row of the movie theater are waiting for you to get up so they can leave, and the people sitting behind you are hoping you'll remain seated so they can continue reading the credits.

113. Any voting system in which you can win the popular vote and lose the election.

114. That it's impossible to say no to a minor cultural event like the Portsmouth Choir's reenactment of the Normandy Invasion without seeming small-minded.

115. The dried globule that forms at the top of lotion dispensers.

116. Noticing that the celebrities whom people say you resemble are always gangly and pale.

117. When you go onto YouTube and three hours later you're watching clips of passengers freaking out in airports.

118. That "You roam the lush forests of my florid heart" has probably been said by someone.

119. Wishing you could blurt out, "Nope—next," each time a waiter starts describing a special you don't like.

120. Feeling neurotic for patting the grease off your pizza with a napkin.

121. When the light turns yellow and you hit the gas and realize that there's no way you'll make it but there's no stopping now!

122. When someone says, "*P* as in 'Paul,'" and you're not sure if she said, "*P* as in 'Paul,'" or, "*B* as in 'ball.'"

123. High fives that don't quite come off right.

124. When someone is simply too physically beautiful not to stare at.

125. Totaling a car that has a full tank of gas.

126. Jobs where they try to make you feel better about your meager salary by giving you a nice title.

127. When you have an anxiety-inducing number of browser tabs open and little willingness to close any of them.

128. Getting a Q at the end of a Scrabble game.

129. When someone asks, "What's up?" and you reply, "Fine, thanks."

130. The fake road scenery that whizzes past drivers in old movies.

131. Listening to your accountant reiterate the tax advantages of losing most of your money.

132. Carrying an item into a store that sells that item.

133. That anyone who says they don't need to pay someone to help them figure out their issues needs to pay someone to help them figure out their issues.

134. That only when space aliens attack our planet will we stop killing one another (we'll focus on the aliens).

135. Boys + toys = noise.

136. The gym teacher you had as a kid who thought his "tough but fair" routine would make you look back on him with gratitude, but whom you still remember as a stained-sweatpants-wearing, overly competitive freak.

137. When your girlfriend, who is sitting on your lap, asks you if she's crushing your legs, and she is.

138. Stumbling over something in front of strangers and immediately having to decide between: (a) ignoring your misstep and trying to walk nonchalantly onward, or (b) looking over your shoulder while making a slightly exaggerated look of annoyance as if to imply, "They really ought to fix that!"

139. When fast food is slow.

Six Annoying Things About Being a School Nurse

—by G. F.

1. Head lice, because they don't make the kids sick, they just make the parents crazy.

2. That because of the President's Council on Fitness, Sports, and Nutrition all of the middle school kids have to go running, even though I know some of them are so out of shape they'll come back injured or unable to breathe.

3. Teachers who send children to the nurse for a paper cut that I can't even find.

4. That students take condoms and I find them later all over the school, filled with water.

5. Teachers who panic over a nosebleed and forget to give the kid a tissue, causing him to bleed all the way to the office.

6. Girls who fake their period to skip swimming.

140. Rekindling nothing as you and your spouse vacation where you honeymooned ten years ago.

141. When you're not sure whether the person on the other end of the phone replied, "Goodbye," so you stay on the line to confirm that she hung up, and after a few seconds of silence she says, "Still there?"

142. When your car gently taps the back of someone else's, and the other driver makes a big production out of "checking for damage."

143. When you tear open a padded envelope, and asbestos-like gray stuff spews into the air.

144. The special class of men who are invited to bachelor parties but not weddings.

145. Wedding toasts that end up being more about the person giving the toast than the bride and groom.

146. Accidentally combining words (e.g., "Oh, absotively").

147. Looking like you're thirty when you're forty, and sixty when you're fifty.

148. Being told, "It's a really stupid show . . . you'll love it."

149. That you don't have the cash to fly on a moment's notice to Japan to bid on Paul's *Sgt. Pepper* uniform.

150. That the only way to truly discover your partner's emotional boundaries is to cross them.

151. Mistaking a Coues's flycatcher for a California condor while bird-watching (not even the same phylum).

152. Peacekeeping missiles.

153. When the grass seems greener on the other side because it is.

154. Writers who strain to avoid using the word "said" (e.g., "How was the pizza?" he solicited. "Too much cheese," she alleged.).

155. When you need to read something that is even smaller than this.

156. That America is the first nation to litter on Mars.

157. TV documentaries in which the narrator pronounces "why" as "hwhy" ("We asked him how many times he had done it . . . and *hwhy!*").

158. Dancing near a group of strangers who aren't welcoming you into their area.

159. When a teenager says, "O*kay* . . . you don't have to *yell*."

160. That navigation apps never say, "In point-one miles, I'll shut the hell up."

161. When you dig up your report cards from grade school and the teachers' comments still ring true (e.g., "Not exactly organized").

162. When your boyfriend experiences "absence makes the heart grow fonder" while you experience "out of sight, out of mind."

163. When winning Most Improved Athlete makes you wonder how bad of an athlete you were.

164. Sending a save-the-date to people you hope won't save the date.

165. When you've got the FBI telling you one thing, the CIA telling you another, and your mom telling you a third.

166. Thinking, *This lady has no clue what she's in for*, as she enthusiastically greets your child on the first day of preschool.

167. The lack of ethnic diversity of hurricane names.

168. People who have a fourth child because they're "already screwed with three."

169. Loud, muffled public announcements ("Ooh ooh unstruh-in in ih aye uh, uh ain ill ee ee aye eye *mahmuhmoomee* ihnuts.").

170. An acidic vomit burp.

171. Late '60s folk songs with ludicrous lyrics (e.g., to a harpsichord and flute playing a sprightly melody, "At dawn we smoke the herb, make one with mother earth, and kiss the napping doves, for to hum a hymn of birth . . .").

172. Having everything except the ability not to take it all for granted.

173. That we don't call models "minus-size," and plus-size models "models."

174. Camping with someone who is high maintenance.

175. When playing Mad Libs with your mom yields the following sentence: "My son's balls are hairy."

176. When it's not funny anymore.

177. Listening to someone who doesn't know how to play piano play piano.

178. When your Wi-Fi connection endlessly defaults to some pricey public hot spot.

179. When the person you'll soon be breaking up with asks to borrow something.

180. Riding a tandem bike alone.

181. Trying to find a way to praise your son who messed up his only line in the school play: "Hark!"

182. My deepest insecurity is (please write neatly):

_____

_____

_____

_____

183. Tipping not because your waiter earned it but because you don't want to look cheap.

184. Sharing a long car ride with a dull acquaintance who isn't comfortable with silence.

185. Biting your cheek on the swollen area where you previously bit it.

186. People who won't let you open the fridge during a power outage.

187. Hoping the person you're kissing will move their tongue in any direction other than jabbing horizontal ovals.

188. The speed with which a marriage can destroy a lifelong friendship.

189. Being unable to keep the kite aloft, while your child sits in the grass, quietly weeping.

190. That you can't maintain a running monologue about each food item the checkout clerk scans for another customer (e.g., "Promotes diabetes," *plip*. "Sodium bomb," *plip*.).

191. Spending every New Year's Eve with your one friend who is perpetually single.

192. That nobody who asks you to "lower it just a tad" really wants you to lower it by only a tad.

193. Being the only one who hasn't reached puberty, when the coach shouts, "Great practice—now let's hit the showers!"

194. Our mission statement—for internal use only: "The dispersion of mercury-infused photovoltaics manufactured by the Remington Buckley Group, whose profits will finance the creation and mass dispersion of fake incendiary social media posts aimed at influencing US presidential elections in order to help Buckley Remington secure a $500 million photovoltaic contract."

195. The people exercising in the gym who look at you through the window, making you feel like an inert mass of flab.

196. When Lincoln Logs fool children into believing it's easy to build a log cabin.

197. Not liking the gift you pulled out of the grab bag as much as the one you put into it.

198. When you hold the ketchup bottle over your french fries and the first thing that comes out is red water.

199. Listening to a detailed explanation of how to do something that you already know how to do.

200. Armrest warfare on an airplane.

201. That your close friend's decision to get married will cost you $75 for an engagement party gift, $100 for the bachelor party or shower, $200 to rent a tuxedo or $300 to buy a dress and shoes you'll never wear again, $200 for the gift, and $500 for airfare if they're having it in Colorado, and suddenly you've blown well over $1,000.

202. People who are afraid to step on an escalat— missed it . . . how 'bout thi . . . no not that one . . . tha— *not that!*

203. Tornadoes that don't harm the people who chase them.

204. That Barry Manilow didn't write his hit song "I Write the Songs."

205. When all your husband wants to do during the third day of your honeymoon is stay in the hotel room and watch the NFL draft.

206. That there are shampoos for "Curl and Shine," "Length and Strength," "Damaged Hair," "Added Bounce," "Intensive Moisturizing," and "Frizz Taming," but none for "Badly Balding."

207. The saying, "A good idea, if well executed, will outperform a great idea that is poorly executed," means little to you when you're someone who rarely has ideas.

208. That it's the people who love you who are the most adept at tormenting you.

209. When you need to mail something and then you see a mailman and wonder if it would be insulting to just hand the envelope to him as if he's some kind of human mailbox.

210. When your reply to a question depends on your comprehension of a word you don't know.

Eight Annoying Things About Being a Comedian/Comedy Writer

—by G. F.

1. Seeing a line you wrote show up on throw pillows, pot holders, and greeting cards.

2. When the comedian who goes on before you covers all the same areas you are planning to cover, but with better punch lines.

3. When family members who have always had doubts that you are funny are sitting in the front row.

PROFESSIONALLY ANNOYED

4. When the comedian who goes on before you does raunchy sex and bodily excretion material, and you must follow with your droll remarks about the presidential hopefuls.

5. When the celebrity who is the centerpiece and punch line of your best joke is suddenly the victim of a tragic illness or accident.

6. Having the bartender decide to blend a new batch of margaritas in the middle of a delicate joke setup.

7. When your best joke makes a high-profile appearance on late-night television without you.

8. When, after all the time and work you put into thinking up new material, someone gets a large advance to write a book full of lists by other people.

211. When the song the venue plays before the musician goes on stage is better than the musician's music.

212. When your car has one of those quiet, high-pitched horns that implies, "It's okay, you can step all over me."

213. A sneeze that lingers in your nose and then absorbs into your forehead.

214. That forty-two seems to be the average age of people who describe themselves as "in their late thirties."

215. Realizing that your favorite part of any event— the office Christmas party, taking your kids to the amusement park—is the food.

216. Error 404: Not found.

217. When the stranger you've been driving behind for hours suddenly exits the highway, making you feel like you've lost a friend.

218. Situations in which you have to read instructions while upside down.

219. Having second thoughts about your first tattoo.

220. Brainstorming with an idiot (e.g., "What if the children make a circus and we have them build robotic elephants?").

221. When your beak is sore from trying to chew a pebble that looks like a nut.

222. When an offhand comment from a child shatters your self-serving delusions.

223. People who feign disinterest in a celebrity sighting.

224. Having to entertain guests moments after learning that the personal scandal you've hidden for some twenty-plus years will soon be made public.

225. That you can return shoes that don't fit right, but no one will take back your sibling.

226. When the most impressive aspect of a concert is the costume changes.

227. Making plans with someone to make plans with them.

228. When someone shakes your hand with a wet hand and says, "It's just water."

229. When a HELP WANTED ad says, SERIOUS CANDIDATES ONLY! as if a glib candidate, upon reading that, would figure they ought not respond.

230. When remembering you spent last Valentine's Day with Andrew makes being alone for this Valentine's Day more palatable.

231. When your waiter asks, "Still picking?" as if you're some kind of bird.

232. The teenage piranha pool known as high school.

233. That there are 525,600 minutes per year and none of them include (reader, please finish this point—I have dinner plans):

_____

_____

_____

234. When you can tell by someone's skeleton that they must have been ugly.

235. Parents who try to make their children's birthday parties educational.

236. That reading a paper newspaper makes you look like a caveman.

237. When a moment of serenity reveals how crazed your life usually is.

238. When someone's social media persona ruins your perception of them.

239. That the dance moves in *Footloose* were mostly gymnastics.

240. The kind of techno new age music that makes you feel like you're getting a massage in a disco spa.

241. When your tongue digs out a chunk of food and you're not sure if you should be repulsed or pleased by this unexpected, slick, post-meal little snack.

242. When restaurants won't give you the lunch special on a weekend.

243. Remembering how people of your current age seemed so old when you were a child.

244. That it's the dogs who have tamed us.

245. That becoming a parent will turn you into a sneak.

246. Tribute albums that feature obscure bands (the Chicken Parms covering "Hey Jude" and the Four Horseguys doing a reggae version of "Let It Be").

247. When the tip of a sausage is all rubbery.

248. Delaying getting out of bed because the room is stupid-cold.

249. That the times when you're least able to deal with hosting a lot of guests—having a baby, losing a loved one—are when you will host the most.

250. When you need to give up your dreams in order to enjoy your life.

251. When being informed makes you seem strange.

252. That when you're young you want to be older, and when you're old you want to be younger, and when you're dead you want to be alive.

253. Meeting the right person at the right time in the wrong outfit.

254. When unpleasant people have an unpleasant conversation.

255. Thank you for reading this book. Please listen carefully as our menu options have changed. For a funny joke, go to number 48. For one of the weaker points in this book, go to 721.

256. Difficult password recovery questions (e.g., "Where do you want to retire?").

257. People who clean because the cleaning lady is coming.

258. That selfies kill more people per year than sharks.

259. Those moments when you have no choice but to sift through a public trash can.

260. Homeschooling. It's hard enough being home parented!

261. Any car commercial that features a sprinting cheetah.

262. When someone wins a million dollars by hitting a half-court shot, and then the promoter tries to avoid paying because the guy stepped on the line.

263. The strands of dead skin that hang from the roof of your mouth after you've scorched it eating microwaved pizza.

264. When a documentary about your life includes the following narration: "But the severe heat and dehydration had taken a terrible toll on his body, and he was no longer able to gain nourishment from his friend's fetid corpse."

265. When your mother-in-law is about to use your computer and you don't know *what* URLs will autofill in the browser.

266. When you like her, and she knows it, and you know she knows it, but she doesn't know you know she knows it or that you know she doesn't know you know she knows it (because she doesn't know—how could she? Why don't you just tell her you know she knows you know she knows?).

267. Auto-play videos that can't be disabled.

268. Assuming that every couple strolling by is happy despite the fact that you sometimes appear happy in your uninspired relationships.

269. When you and your friend's fiancée have yet to reach the point where you stop pretending to like each other.

270. That your last moment of unqualified glory was in Little League thirty-one years ago.

271. The unfortunate unfashionability of earmuffs.

272. The slow admission to yourself over a period of many years that you'll never have a good body.

273. One-hour commute × 2 commutes per day × 5 workdays per week = 10 hours commuting per week. Ten hours of commuting per week × 50 weeks = 500 hours commuting per year. Five hundred hours commuting per year × 45 years = 22,500 hours, or 2.57 years of your life spent commuting.

274. That pharmacies don't have a "Staff Recommends" section (e.g., *"Fruit-Eze Stool Softener is my favorite. Perfect consistency."—Harold*).

275. When you enter a space-time continuum devoid of color and sound.

276. Trying to insert a three-pronged plug into a two-pronged outlet.

277. When lice lay larvae in your daughter's hair.

278. When your mom calls you by your corny childhood nickname in front of your friends (e.g., "Hi, Chipwich!").

279. When the one thing you have a passion for is destroying your health.

280. Sensing that your opponent is more interested in physically harming you than winning.

281. That if you're around toddlers long enough you'll eventually find yourself saying, "Excuse me, those are my privates."

282. That perfecting doo-wop harmonies with your buddies on street corners is really not an option for you.

283. People who don't remove their Christmas decorations until spring.

284. When someone you're not really with breaks up with you.

285. The expression, "It is what it is." Did you think I might have suspected it was something else?

Six Annoying Things About Being a Feature Film Casting Director

—*by E. L. and J. T.*

1. When a director or producer tells you that her daughter doesn't think an actor is cute enough.

2. Auditioning actors who, after shaking your hand with a sweaty palm, tell you they have the flu.

3. Being called a casting *agent*.

4. When your relatives ask you why you cast a particular actor, whom they hated in the movie.

5. When the actors take it too far in auditions by vigorously miming their physical actions, like pretending to urinate or drive a car.

6. When actors tell you a little too much about their personal lives.

286. That celebrities who are fairly new to their fame often consult more established celebrities for advice on how to handle celebrity, and that you belong to neither of these groups.

287. When the closest you come to achieving your dream of having a pool is a dented plastic kiddie pool filled with brown water by the side of your house.

288. People who have no clue how loudly they talk.

289. When your father tells a long, meandering joke to the waitress, who is holding a heavy tray, and then mistakes her obligatory laugh for a real one.

290. Wanting to fix a stranger's half-curled collar.

291. When a difficult adult is told she was a difficult baby.

292. That it's no longer acceptable for sailors to skip down the street whistling show tunes.

293. When missing the bus by twenty seconds plunges you into a deep pit of self-reproach.

294. That there isn't a restaurant that uses dogs as friendly waiters and a cat as a snooty maître d'.

295. Wondering, based on his answers, if the person you're copying from knows less than you.

296. When the car driving behind you has a ski rack attached to the top, making it look like a police car in your rearview mirror.

297. That plastic surgeons earn more than heart surgeons.

298. Realizing, while trying to beat your kid in Chutes and Ladders, that you are the competitive creep you've always been accused of being.

299. Missing work the one day your boss doesn't show.

300. That you can't wear leather pants convincingly.

301. That the greatest expression of love you'll receive is at your funeral.

302. People who insist that celery has no taste.

303. Wondering, after using "it's not you, it's me" to end a relationship, if it *is* in fact you.

304. Being unable to feel where the clear tape starts as you keep gliding your fingertip around the roll.

305. When every action of every person around you seems absurd (e.g., a man yanking 300 napkins from a napkin dispenser, a woman texting while the cashier waits to take her order, etc.).

306. Overhearing someone whisper, "Who is that clown?" as you walk into a party.

307. People who emit the *ha-eenh!* sound while trying to hold in a sneeze.

308. When a celebrity who's had plastic surgery says he's open to having plastic surgery.

309. Being unable to relate to woodcut illustrations of Pilgrim women weaving.

310. Recalling the misery that we put our substitute teachers through.

311. That no one will ever care to distinguish between your "early work" and your "later periods."

312. Being convinced that everyone named Lucas is part of a vile race of aliens sent here from a very mean place.

313. Seeing shoes of every color, brand, and style in your girlfriend's suitcase as you struggle to close the zipper.

314. Lead singer leg kicks.

315. Driving by a stranded car with someone standing beside it on the side of the highway and feeling bad for that person, but not bad enough to pull over and help.

316. People whose contributions to legal discussions consist of things like, "He oughta fry!"

317. Amusement park fatigue.

318. When, after a hefty meal, an abrasive friend of your parents slaps you on the back and says, "You sure can really pack it in, eh?"

319. When even a passing stranger can look at the two of you and tell that your relationship is failing.

320. When there's nothing you want to do but you don't want to do nothing.

321. That being a narcissistic jerk is an evolutionarily positive trait.

322. When something is funny but you don't know why it's funny (e.g., "2 + 2 = 4 ha!" is funny).

323. That 3 + 3 = 6 ha! is funnier than 2 + 2 = 4 ha!

324. Adult birthday zealotry that lacks irony.

325. When you tell friends that you're getting divorced and they all start trashing your spouse.

326. That we judge balding men by the choices they make in coping with their baldness.

327. Thinking, *No one is ever going to find my bones.*

328. When the new friends you want to impress are breaking the law.

329. When a twenty-two-year-old quits his job because it "isn't interesting enough."

330. When the smell of a lit banana nut bread candle makes you hungry.

331. People whose self-confidence depends upon a lack of self-knowledge.

332. When disgusting feet wear sandals.

333. That it's illegal to text and drive but there's no law to stop you from folding your laundry from behind the wheel.

334. Having to choose between physical and financial health.

335. Taking an SAT prep class early in the morning after a night of binge drinking and projectile vomiting.

336. When a toddler swipes a computer screen with his finger as if it were a smartphone.

337. Being the only one to know that something is meaningless.

338. Anytime a movie preview says, "And introducing . . ." as if you should suddenly think of this person as a star.

339. That being in a relationship causes you to be invited to twice as many lame events.

340. When you have a garage sale and a neighbor decides to throw a few items on his front lawn.

341. When an eco-friendly company is rude to humans.

342. When you want to leave a restaurant but they've already given you bread and water.

343. Knowing you're in the picture a stranger is taking.

344. When you're livin' the dream and the dream's a nightmare.

345. That babies are essentially randomly set human alarm clocks with broken snooze buttons.

346. Hi, I'm Scott Cohen and I approve of this message.

347. When a teacher says that there is no such thing as a stupid question, and then a student raises his hand and asks a stupid question.

348. When a car trails behind you in the parking lot as you walk to your car.

349. When a Martian waddles into your kitchen, touches your forearm with its felp, suctions its cool, gummy fliggums onto your forehead, and starts spraying shaboowy zam zam into your face.

350. When your face appears on TV and at the bottom of the screen it says, *Believes he is mentally stable.*

351. When you're having a bad day and then something bad happens.

352. When an unhealthy relationship that is too much fun to quit turns into a healthy relationship that is too boring to maintain.

353. People who vote undecided.

354. When you intentionally leave late because the person you have plans with is always late, and you still end up arriving twenty minutes earlier than he does.

355. That few things can please a toddler as much as an underwater fart.

Five Annoying Things About Working at a Café

—by A. N.

1. People who try to pronounce "croissant" with a French accent.

2. Customers who ask for a "regular coffee."

3. People who are texting or talking on their phone when it's their turn to order, then resent it when I skip to the next person in line.

4. Yuppies who think they're adventurous for ordering lattes with flavor shots.

5. Escorting customers to the restroom and unlocking the door fifty-six times a day.

356. Being subtly manipulated by algorithms that monitor your every click.

357. Men who take their shirts off before getting into a fight. Wouldn't you rather keep it on and maybe add a helmet and some elbow pads?

358. When you bring pie to a party but it isn't served.

359. People who can't sit in the opposite direction that the train is moving in.

360. Vacationing with a couple that bickers.

361. Having to instantly applaud and act all happy after it's announced during a televised ceremony that one of the four other nominees just won the Academy Award.

362. When someone keeps bumping you with the overstuffed backpack they're wearing.

363. When being with the wrong person feels lonelier than being alone.

364. When your hair defies logic, space, and time.

365. When the flavor of the day is the same all week.

366. Trying to get a key off a key chain without losing a fingernail.

367. Sexual positions that make you think, *Whatever happens do not fart.*

368. When all the neighbors talk longingly about the person who lived in your home before you (enough about Sachi and her '80s-themed parties).

369. Bicyclists who use hand signals. Okay, you're about to turn left. Congratulations.

370. The second-to-last day of a vacation.

371. The vulnerability you feel while sitting on a public toilet.

372. When accidentally hitting "reply all" creates a lifelong rift between two of your closest friends.

373. When you can't twist off the lid from a jar and someone else can.

374. The average human falls asleep in only fourteen minutes. Many people, upon reading this statistic, ponder it each night in bed, making it more difficult for them to fall asleep. Perhaps you are one of them.

375. Injecting needless spite into family situations.

376. Having to examine a map publicly in a foreign country.

377. People who rationalize, "I'm a better person for it," after every negative experience—you are never a better person for having lost your wallet.

378. When the discovery of new mental disorders interferes with your ability to enjoy the ones you have already.

379. Wondering who was rude enough to leave an empty roll of toilet paper and then remembering it was you.

380. That those guys combing beaches with metal detectors never actually find anything of value.

381. Hearing your name announced at the airport.

382. When someone jogs by at seven a.m. while you walk home from another all-night drinking episode.

383. When a toddler asks you twenty-three minutes into the flight to Australia, "Are we almost there yet?"

384. How the commercialization of Christmas forces Jews to give more expensive gifts for Hanukkah.

385. When you first started dating, you found it cute that he enjoys hunting and you prefer creating mosaic tile designs, but now it's not so funny that you have little in common.

386. When you refrain from mocking a professional athlete at a game because you fear he'll pummel you.

387. Eating a turkey sub alone in your apartment on Thanksgiving Day.

388. That the inventor of the spork is wealthy, while the inventor of the foon lives a life of modest obscurity.

389. Having to gush over every aspect of your friend's new home.

390. Wondering how to convey to the well-meaning woman on the train who just said, "Cheer up," the extent to which your life has fallen apart.

391. Kissing hello the people you wouldn't have invited to your surprise party.

392. Wishing you could look and feel the way you looked and felt when you were younger, even though an older version of you will one day wish you could look and feel the way you currently look and feel.

393. When all the pigeons stop what they're doing and look at you like you're completely insane.

394. That if aliens abducted you and returned you to Earth radically enlightened, whatever you could contribute to the sum of mankind's knowledge would be ignored.

395. When the person you're eating with wipes her mouth, causing you to wonder if you need to wipe your mouth.

396. When your therapist tells you, "Generally, brilliant people struggle to find happiness, and it works the other way around too, and certainly you're no exception to this rule," leaving you to wonder whether he means you're unhappy or dumb.

397. When the subtitles in a movie are the same color as the background.

398. When the amount of time it takes you to get over your ex exceeds the amount of time you were actually with your ex.

399. Showing up to an empty restaurant with a reservation.

400. When the media accuses the media of being irresponsible.

401. Pondering whether to tell your friend that you've had sex with the guy you're setting her up with.

402. That everything but human nature seems to evolve.

403. Having your first bargaining offer accepted, leaving you to wonder whether you could have done better.

404. When you sell an extra concert ticket to a stranger on the internet and end up sitting next to him. When handling customer complaints for a West Coast–based company entails fielding calls from angry New Yorkers at six a.m.

405. Thought that was a typo? Shame on you.

406. Sitting in traffic with the people you're trying to get away from.

407. When you put a kid in time-out and she refuses to show an iota of disappointment.

408. When both of you pretend that neither of you saw a piece of food fly out of your mouth while you were talking.

409. That cows and drunken frat boys are the only mammals who can urinate backward.

410. Celebrity impersonators who don't give up the bit offstage.

411. When your child's first full sentence is, "I bit Peter."

412. The message of a D-minus: Nothing would have pleased me more than to have failed you, but you didn't quite stink enough.

413. Not knowing at what point in January it becomes inappropriate to wish someone Happy New Year.

414. When no one witnesses you nail an impossibly tight parallel park.

415. Crouton disappointment.

416. Incompetent walkers who step directly into where you're headed.

417. Knowing you'll be sleeping over at the house of the person you've started dating but feeling funny about bringing a change of clothing.

418. When you open a bag of microwavable popcorn and the steam nearly melts your fingertips.

419. Praying that you don't get aroused during your massage.

420. That there's no sound—perhaps *zwamp!* or *veezeyack!*—that can instantly silence your dad.

421. When the flushing of a toilet causes your shower to have terrifying temperature swings.

422. When you take a toddler to the bookstore and she only wants to read the books she has at home.

423. A failure of government at every level.

424. When your teenage son has a few friends over for a "snack" and they pretty much clear out the entire kitchen.

425. When you're like, *Why am I attracted to that old lady?* and then you're like, *Oh, because I'm an old man.*

426. When you're told that in the first several seconds following the big bang the universe cooled from 1,784,000,000,000 degrees to 1,342,000 degrees, and the most intelligent response you can muster is, "It really cooled a lot."

427. How deceptive one's height can be while they're sitting.

428. When children mockingly imitate you and it's accurate.

429. That your groin generally puts its interests in front of yours.

430. That your groin generally puts its interests in front of yours. (This point bears repeating.)

Five Annoying Things About Being a Hairstylist

—*by L. V.*

1. People who ask me to do what I want and cut as much as I want, then say it's too short when I only cut off an inch.

2. When clients decide they're going to highlight their own hair with Jolen Creme Bleach the day before they have to attend a wedding, and then proceed to freak out when you can't fit them in for an emergency six-hour color correction.

3. Clients who constantly touch their hair or move around in order to make eye contact with you during their cut.

4. People who tell you how they want you to hold their hair as you cut it, and which scissors to use. Hey, I'm the one who paid for beauty school.

5. When clients show me a picture of some gorgeous model and ask to look like her when they are five feet tall and have overtreated, damaged hair.

431. Preachy vegetarians.

432. Trying to avoid eye contact with the guy at the urinal next to you, as he tries to do the same.

433. Those moments when your life depends on getting twenty grand, any kind of vehicle you can get your hands on, and a fake passport.

434. The difference between the scenes in the travel brochures and your vacations.

435. That mankind hasn't figured out how to harness the obsessive anxiety of planning a wedding into a viable energy source.

436. When someone wins the $100 million lotto and says it won't affect their lifestyle.

437. Tipping a bartender for handing you a bottle of beer but giving nothing to the guy who pumps your gas in the pouring rain.

438. That you'll never again be a child who can fall asleep in the back seat, feeling completely safe while your parents drive you home.

439. Rearranging heavy furniture, then realizing you liked it better before.

440. Losing track of time in the diner's restroom and coming out to find everyone huddled under the counter, gagged and bound.

441. When neither of you is attracted to the other, yet you continue removing each other's clothing.

442. That anxiety over a pregnancy scare can cause a woman to get her period later than normal.

443. Texting while walking.

444. People who don't pronounce the letter *H* (e.g., "The portions are euge!").

445. When your heart skips a beat, reminding you of its eventual failure.

446. Putting an I SUPPORT THE LOCAL POLICE sticker on your car, as if that will somehow save you from getting a ticket.

447. When a work meeting becomes a gripe fest.

448. Feeling so bored during retirement you actually miss the job you hated.

449. Gas tanks that are empty the moment they hit "Empty."

450. Software updates that slow down your phone, forcing you to buy a new one.

451. The futility of going back to sleep in an attempt to finish a great dream.

452. When a teacher erases the entire blackboard but misses one mark.

453. When your fear of forgetting a vital piece of information forces you to keep repeating it in your mind (e.g., *Don't forget the passports, don't forget the passports, don't forget . . .*).

454. Not knowing whether you're supposed to abide by the twenty-five-mile-per-hour school zone speed limit on weekends.

455. Realizing you were wearing the same outfit the last time you hung out with this person.

456. When your Seeing Eye dog goes blind.

457. Child guards on lighters and aspirin containers that make you feel like an imbecile.

458. Songs that give you unsettling flashbacks to your dentist's reception area.

459. When someone asks, "Do you think it's stuffy in here?" when they really mean, "Can you open the freakin' window?"

460. Receiving parenting advice from someone who isn't a parent.

461. Stoking the fire for your girlfriend at the ski chalet and ending up with a room full of smoke.

462. That you can't slap-drum the beat of "Billie Jean" on the thighs of the stranger seated next to you.

463. People who make you wonder if freedom of speech is a good thing.

464. Realizing the company softball game is going to be a lighthearted affair instead of a competitive game in which you could finally prove what a stud athlete you are.

465. Having an acute inner-anal itch in public.

466. When being alone in an elevator with someone you haven't kissed but want to kiss makes you feel like you're in fifth grade.

467. Being unable to stop analyzing whether you stepped into the longer of the two lines.

468. When a seat is hot from a stranger's butt-warmth.

469. Listening to medical students get the answers wrong as they quiz one another in a café.

470. When achieving a lifelong goal makes you feel inexplicably sad.

471. When your plan to supplant the eggplant you planted doesn't pan out as planned.

472. That either you find the past or it finds you.

473. People who say, "I could care less" when they mean that they couldn't care less.

474. When you order something different to "change it up a little" and then regret not getting what you always get.

475. Men who think if they just keep talking to a woman, she'll become interested.

476. That the first thing you do when you look at a photo is see if you're in it and, if so, how you look.

477. When you love someone more than you like them.

478. Wading through a large, motionless group of people.

479. When your situation is so hopeless that the best your family and friends can offer for encouragement is, "Everything will work itself out."

480. When your trip to Paris ruins your hometown bakery.

481. DJs who, as a song ends, thoughtfully repeat its most clichéd line as if it's profound.

482. People who figure that getting married will resolve their partner's annoying habits.

483. Trying to find a sincere Mother's Day card that isn't too sentimental.

484. That every time you try to impart wisdom to your son, he continues to stare into a screen.

485. Cutesy product names that misuse the letter Z (e.g., Cheez Doodles).

486. When your hosts can hear your urine splashing into the toilet.

487. A brochure on your windshield that looks like a parking ticket.

488. The contempt the other magicians show you because you reveal how the tricks are done.

489. That it's impossible to ask someone how he likes his meal without it being interpreted as a hint that you'd like a bite.

490. When your spouse tells two of the same three stories every time you go out to eat with another couple.

491. People who stop telling a story "because it's too disgusting to tell during dinner," leaving you to try to envision what was so disgusting about it.

492. When air blasts out of a tire as you connect the pump to inflate it.

493. The viselike grip that a select group of men holds on the world's riches.

494. How painful a pimple is when it's located directly below your nostril.

495. Wondering if your students find history as historically inaccurate as you do.

496. That the commercials are louder than the programs.

497. How nasty the fifth mozzarella stick tastes.

498. When the most memorable thing about sex is how forgettable it was.

499. Wondering if your ex, whom you're still obsessing over, has forgotten you as quickly as you've forgotten all your other exes.

500. When you yell, "Has anyone seen my wallet?" and someone calls out, "It's wherever you left it."

501. Publicly struggling to get your arm into your coat.

Seven Annoying Things About Being a Personal Trainer

—by K. M.

1. When a client pulls a microscopic piece of flab on her thighs and asks, "What exercise can I do to get rid of this one little squidge right here?"

2. People who come in with really, really offensive BO or extreme perfume.

3. Guys who pick a bench and sit and read a newspaper for twenty minutes.

4. "You know, I'm in really good shape even though I haven't been to the gym in more than two years."

5. People who sing along to their music.

6. People who think they're cool because they sweat a lot.

7. Guys who get all territorial about machines.

502. Any menu item described as "gently nestled."

503. When your three-year-old mimics everything your five-year-old does, and currently your five-year-old is kicking your six-year-old.

504. When all your coworkers resent you for being voted "Employee of the Month" two months in a row.

505. Liking the *whoosh* sound of a pool cue being swung.

506. When every thought, each micromovement of your fingers, is focused on some pointless act, like bending a deformed paper clip back into shape.

507. When the first sip of orange juice reminds you that you've recently brushed your teeth.

508. Noticing that you answered "true" for nine of the ten questions on an exam and wondering if maybe you should change a few "true"s to "false."

509. When a child's idea of cleaning up is playing with the mess.

510. Discovering a new talent that will never be of any benefit to you.

511. Forgetting in which situations that "which" is supposed to be used instead of "that."

512. That potato chips nowadays seem to be made of anything other than potato.

513. When you break up with your boyfriend and end up missing his family more than you miss him.

514. When a chicken nugget is a crunchy, gray amalgamation of assorted chicken bits.

515. The perverse pleasure we get from watching cell phone videos of natural disasters.

516. The stench of the cheese section in a fancy supermarket.

517. Lunatics whose lunacy is only discernible after you've moved in with them.

518. Watching the bar mitzvah band on its break, as they wolf down hors d'oeuvres at a little table in the back.

519. Sensing that the truck you rented might not fit under the approaching overpass.

520. When you meet your girlfriend's friends for the first time and know, as you get up to use the restroom, that they'll be talking about you.

521. When you give the right answer during class and your teacher responds, "Good for you!" which you and your classmates decipher as, "Congratulations, doofus, you finally got one right."

522. When your eyes instinctively dart to the side because the man sitting nearby caught you staring at him, heightening your urge to look again. So you slowly pan your eyes back, only to be caught again, further intensifying your desire to peek one last time.

523. Wondering if you are entitled to the deep sense of loss you feel when a celebrity dies.

524. After waiting twenty-eight minutes to see your doctor, a nurse brings you to a room—where you wait another twenty-eight minutes.

525. The moment between dry heaves when you realize another heave is coming.

526. When they put a scoop of ice cream on your cone but none in it.

527. That Valentine's Day was placed in February— just in case single people have recovered from Christmas and New Year's Eve.

528. When they arrest someone for successfully climbing a skyscraper.

529. When a houseguest treats you like the proprietor of a bed and breakfast.

530. Waking up from a long nap at 10:18 p.m.

531. When someone asks if you notice anything different about them and you don't.

532. Buying something not because you want it but because you're tired of convincing yourself not to buy it.

533. That being in a relationship is like having a full-time job and being alone is like being unemployed.

534. When a politician begins his sentences with "frankly" or "in all candor."

535. People who think they can cut the line because they have a minor question.

536. Having unlimited access to the things that bore you.

537. People who immediately stand up when the plane lands as if they're going somewhere.

538. Multi multitasking because you're beyond beyond-slammed.

539. Not knowing the difference between a lake and a pond (is there one?).

540. Falling up a flight of stairs.

541. When you think you've found a parking spot only to realize that a short car is tucked in there.

542. Cold hand sex.

543. Thinking of the perfect response you could have used in an argument a few minutes after it ended.

544. That it's easier for artificial intelligence to detect a nipple than hate speech.

545. That your supervisor only seems to stop by your cubicle when you are shopping online.

546. When a hot celebrity claims she was a nerd in high school.

547. When saying goodbye to everyone takes nearly an hour.

548. When you say something benign—e.g., "I need to put my pork in your slow cooker"—and it comes off as perverted.

549. That when writers are paid by the word, they tend to write sentences that are perhaps a tad longer than they really need to be, kindest of readers.

550. When you become the very thing you mocked.

551. When someone in a bad mood accuses you of being in a bad mood.

552. People who retire at the age of forty not because they made millions but because they're cheap bastards.

553. When your biggest tormenter is also your greatest ally.

554. When sitting in traffic causes you to hit more traffic.

555. *Careful, the beverage you're about to enjoy is extremely hot.* Yes, it's called coffee.

556. When you're sitting in the passenger seat and a car comes speeding toward you, causing your leg to stomp on an imaginary break.

557. What your husband turns into when his college buddies stop by.

558. That the only time your ex thinks of you is when she realizes that she hasn't thought of you in ages.

559. When a mass murderer defends himself in court and does a surprisingly competent job.

560. Not wanting to spend the crisp, brand-new dollar bills you've just been handed.

561. When they ask you to only clap once at a graduation ceremony.

562. How rarely you get to say "trolley." It's a great little word. Go ahead, say it. No, don't think it, *say* it.

563. When rocking a baby to sleep has more of an effect on you than the baby.

564. When you're on some dull family vacation as a child and everywhere you go you hope to find someone else who is going through the same thing, who is ready to pull you from it all and show you something beautiful and profound.

565. Using your phone as a social crutch.

566. Enduring a caning from a vicious prep school headmaster in New England in 1925.

567. Feeling a shameful jolt of joy upon reading a sign that says, PLEASE DO NOT TIP.

568. That you're not paid to discover new ice cream flavors.

569. When you're exhausted and horny and have to choose between exhausted sex or horny sleep.

570. That point in a relationship where it's kind of wrong to mess around elsewhere, but not yet completely wrong.

571. When someone opens his car door at a red light and dumps some coffee onto the road.

572. Needing to display the garish housewarming gift someone gave you every time they come over.

573. When you get an early wake-up call at a hotel, and they expect you to say "hello."

574. When a person at the table next to yours asks what you're eating and then orders something else.

575. That more people would listen to Kylie Jenner than leading health experts.

576. Believing that the only reason someone exists is to try to drive you insane.

577. When a toddler walks around barking demands.

578. When the only reason something is meaningful to you is because it once had meaning.

579. When someone tells you his phone number and puts a "one" in front of the area code.

580. When neither you nor the guy working the cash register can remember if you handed him a ten- or twenty-dollar bill.

581. You know how some people close jars too tightly? Well, there are also people who don't close them tightly enough, and that's not much fun either!

Five Annoying Things About Being a Voice-Over Artist

—by H. P.

1. When I put the headphones on for the first time and they're all sweaty.

2. Trying to make a prescription drug's side effects sound attractive.

3. Having to manufacture a cute chuckle on cue for a baby wipe commercial.

4. When the client says, "That was perfect," and they record it fifty more times "just to be safe."

5. When you're recording something that you thought was important and everyone in the booth, including the recording engineer, is eating lunch and paying no attention.

582. Distant relatives whom you see at the same holiday function every year, with whom you pretend to have a real relationship.

583. How little a postcard says.

584. When you're not sure if the people roaming around your foggy backyard in blue jackets are real.

585. When you try to propose at a rock concert and your girlfriend can't hear you.

586. When scorching sand causes you to run with doe-like leaps.

587. When you feel glum and someone asks, "What's wrong?" causing you to answer in a high-pitched voice, "Nothing!"

588. How hard it is to fold fitted sheets.

589. When your boyfriend promises to cook you a romantic dinner—but when you get to his place, he comes to the door with a video game controller in his hand and mutters something about making a quick run to the supermarket "and maybe doing some stir-fry."

590. When everyone knows that the only reason you weren't the last one picked is that your best friend is one of the captains.

591. When you wake up in the dark and the person next to you is crying.

592. When your pet knows more about your needs than you do.

593. Hearing your father slur over the phone, "First I'm up, then I'm down a little, then I'm down a little more. Bing, bang, boom—next thing you know, I'm a hundred grand in the hole!"

594. When a stranger continues sniffling every few seconds but doesn't blow his nose.

595. Forgetting to dodge that nasty pothole at the entrance of Exit 12.

596. When the only shameful thing you've ever done shows up under an internet search of your name.

597. That even the fanciest restaurants suffer from pest-control problems.

598. That you've never been sure what a "Yankee Doodle Dandy" is.

599. When you have your heart broken and it makes you miss the first person who broke your heart.

600. The unusually large number of strangers who crowd around and stare at you as you're lifted into an ambulance.

601. Having to accept number 602 for what it is.

602.

603. The heavy-handed way movie characters are introduced to the audience (e.g., "Neil, is that your younger brother, Tom?").

604. Thank-you notes from babies, e.g.:

Dear Auntie Kim,

Thank you so much for the Dr. Seuss books. I can't wait till I'm old enough to read them! You're so thoughtful!!!

Lots of hugs,
Shannon

605. Owning an introverted dog.

606. Realizing that strangers watched you try to push open a door that reads PULL.

607. Trying not to think about what you're thinking about.

608. The lack of rehearsing that occurs at a rehearsal dinner.

609. When the total comes to "nineteen eighty-seven" and the guy behind you in line says, "Heck of a year!"

610. Socks that lose their elasticity.

611. Looking at yourself in the mirror on the morning of the day in which you're fated to get into a car accident and having no idea what awaits.

612. When your parents, in an effort to boost your self-esteem, convince you that you're a gifted soccer player.

613. Pleasant-looking people who are rude.

614. When you're arguing with an employee and you say, "Let me speak with the manager," and she replies, "I am the manager."

615. Finding it difficult to stop staring at a mannequin's well-shaped chest.

616. When a guy on a bicycle keeps passing you in traffic.

617. When your main concern, moments before dying, is how you look.

618. How men handle having a cold.

619. When all you want is to be fired so you can collect unemployment, and you can't even accomplish that.

620. When the task you've been putting off for two years takes three minutes to complete.

621. Being cognizant of your chewing during a date.

622. Not being sure in what direction to put on a hospital gown.

623. The isolation of being the only person to survive a full-scale nuclear war.

624. The ways women justify purchasing uncomfortable shoes (e.g., "I'll only wear them when we take cabs!").

625. That you never hear, "Due to a decreased volume of calls, hold times will be shorter than expected."

626. Only recognizing happiness through the distorted lens of remembrance.

627. Men who get more aroused from washing their car than their wife.

628. People who order by saying, "Gimme . . ."

629. When a bowling alley is only willing to hold one of your shoes.

630. Dating someone with the personality of a boiled chicken.

631. That the person who invests your money is called a "broker."

632. Hiding from the United States government.

633. When you're not sure if you've launched the vessel of your soul into serene nothingness or you're moored on the shores of eternal bliss (in other words, you've smoked too much weed).

634. That no good occurs after one a.m.

635. The stress of picking a seat while eating in a restaurant with a large group.

636. Wondering if chest pain is causing anxiety or if anxiety is causing chest pain.

637. When someone asks if they can pick your brain. No, you cannot pick my brain.

638. That we tell creative kids that they are dyslexic or they have ADHD, but there's nothing called BCS (Boring Child Syndrome).

639. When a movie preview starts off as a thriller, turns into a romantic comedy, and proves to be a science fiction film.

640. Having an urge to smell odd objects (e.g., a stranger's pocketbook, your mother-in-law's hair, etc.).

641. How weird you feel during the first week of a new job.

642. That courting a person nowadays entails swiping their face from a screen.

643. When a toddler does everything in her power to disturb your few crumbs of peace.

644. When the only people attracted to you are older than anyone you've ever been attracted to.

645. Trying to get a dog to adhere to daylight saving time.

646. The fact that $111,111,111 \times 111,111,111 = 12,345,678,987,654,321$ has done nothing to reduce your student debt.

647. That when you go to a dumb movie, usually the previews are dumb too.

648. Waking up with your arm numb and thinking, *This time it's paralyzed.*

649. When you both finally admit to each other that it just isn't going to work out and then you start getting along great.

650. When words robotically come out of you in response to the mindless small talk a stranger makes (Stranger: "Sure is warm out today." You: "Yes. It is humid.").

651. When the restaurant's slow service forces you to eat like an animal to get back to the office on time.

652. The stage of a relationship when you don't feel comfortable not having sex.

653. When the smell of an indoor pool elicits a rush of painful memories.

654. When a party instinctively segregates into groups who already knew each other.

655. When a school play is more boring than you had expected it to be, and you expected it to be pretty f@$#'n boring.

Five Annoying Things About Being a Company's IT Person

—by J. A.

1. When I've tried everything I know to fix a computer problem, and I beg my supervisor to come, and he taps about two keys and the problem is fixed.

2. When, in order to show my supervisor what's wrong, I go through the steps to make the problem happen again and it doesn't happen.

3. When a coworker has a computer problem and as soon as I get there

PROFESSIONALLY ANNOYED

I know they've already restarted the computer, so the problem is no longer there. But when I ask them if they restarted the computer, they look at me innocently, and say, "Huh? I didn't do anything! I didn't restart it. I haven't touched it since the problem happened."

4. When a coworker stops me in a hallway as I'm on my way home (finally) and asks me to help him with a problem because it will only take five minutes, as if I've got the word "sucker" written on my chest.

5. Fixing the computer of the person who flagged me down after five p.m., and hearing him say, "Okay, I'm calling it a day. I really appreciate your help. See you tomorrow."

656. When all the ranch hands openly snicker at you even though you own the place.

657. When the digital sign above a highway reads NORMAL TRAFFIC CONDITIONS as you sit in bumper-to-bumper traffic.

658. Wondering if a past injury that hasn't healed fully will linger for the rest of your life.

659. When your five-year-old grandson teaches you how to use your phone.

660. When there are a lot of mosquitoes and you're not sure whether to say, "I'm going to put Off on" or, "I'm going to put on Off."

661. People who pronounce "verbiage" as "verbage."

662. Being the last person to stop applauding.

663. Not wanting the money you put into a tip jar to go unnoticed but not wanting to seem like you're trying to be seen doing it.

664. The criminal feeling you get while sneaking six shirts into the fitting room because they have a "five-item limit."

665. People who wave their hand in front of your face while you're staring peacefully into space.

666. That a world of only women would have basically zero violence.

667. Getting sick on a vacation that you used sick days for.

668. That there's no way to apply a computer's "undo" function to your personal life.

669. When finding your roach traps empty adds to your fear that they're not working instead of reassuring you that you don't have roaches anymore.

670. When you go out of your way to let another driver cut into your lane and he doesn't wave thanks.

671. The lingering suspicion each time you lather up with "2-in-1 shampoo plus conditioner" that it isn't as effective as applying shampoo and conditioner separately.

672. Laughing out loud at the movie you went to see alone.

673. When three years into your marriage, your husband's gut really starts taking off.

674. Not being able to look the woman who cleans your hotel room in the eye because of the colossal mess you left.

675. That nearly every square inch of Manhattan has been urinated on at one time or another.

676. When your wish, as you blow out the candles, is that this be the last birthday you spend with these people.

677. Channeling your frustration into a wild burst of consumerism.

678. When your well-to-do seventy-year-old aunt refuses to date men her age because "all they're looking for is a nurse with a purse."

679. When a registry only has absurdly expensive items or a six-dollar wooden spoon.

680. That most cuddling positions become uncomfortable.

681. That it's no longer considered cool to wander through the woods and carve *ZEP RULES* onto large rocks.

682. Wishing you could belly flop onto the cool tile floor and sigh like a dog.

683. When your daughter's boyfriend refers to her saliva as "love nectar."

684. When a deli includes the weight of your plastic container while calculating the cost of your salad bar lunch.

685. When an asteroid crashes into an active volcano blanketing the earth and its every living being with hot, molten lava.

686. That Hawaiian pizza began in Canada.

687. That if you search "jdhfdu" on the internet, something, I'm sure, will appear.

688. When a stunning discovery about mankind's origins receives less attention than the latest sex scandal.

689. When someone demands specific reasons for why you broke up with them.

690. Mr. Constant Lane Changer.

691. Finding it hard to concentrate knowing that a coworker is on vacation.

692. When a restaurant includes the tip without telling you.

693. Joking about something because it's too uncomfortable not to.

694. That it's the normal people who are the weirdest, though the weird ones are pretty weird too.

695. Recalling the days when flying was a pleasant, lighthearted affair.

696. Using your mom's toilet and picturing her boyfriend's jiggly butt touching the very surface you're sitting upon.

697. When they try to make a sixty-year-old actor look twenty-five during flashback scenes.

698. Not being able to remember all the names of the people you've hooked up with.

699. That childhood bullies are often successful later in life.

700. Watching a concert performance online in which the guy who filmed it sings along.

701. When you're waiting to enter the train and all the doors open except for the one in front of you.

702. When your job is a means to an end and that end isn't being met.

703. When you don't know what to do with your hands.

704. When a car pulls over and the driver asks you how to get to such and such place, and you're like, *What is this, 1985?*

705. Celebrities who enter professional poker tournaments and win.

706. There's something I need to tell you but you have to promise not to get mad.

707. People who place their objects on the seats surrounding them.

708. When someone stresses the importance of looking people in the eye, causing you to awkwardly look into his eyes.

709. Sexual tension with a coworker that slowly intensifies for seventeen years.

710. When you should be crying but you're not and you want to but you can't.

711. Eating dinner in a Chinese restaurant with all the other Jews you saw at the movies on Christmas.

712. Having to choose an outfit that will suffice for both work and a date afterward.

713. A lifelong fear of popular girls.

714. Regretting missing an event that you would've regretted going to had you gone.

715. Being outsmarted by an insect.

716. When you refrigerate leftovers from a restaurant and the sauce turns into globs of gloop, glop, and gleep.

717. That working out requires doing extra laundry.

718. How no one ever says, "Hi, Dad," into the camera.

719. That Hollywood can never quite capture the sound of someone's face being punched.

720. Plummeting down a subfreezing sheer mountain ice face in the dark of night.

721. When your shoelace rips far from home.

722. When sleeping while you're sick feels like a 100-hour plotless movie.

723. Audiences who enjoy being scolded by the performer.

724. People who do some kind of yoga pose in every photo.

725. That the sound of your computer's recycling bin being emptied is the same length regardless of whether there's one file or one thousand files.

726. When your imaginary roommate stops paying his share of the rent.

727. "Evaporated cane juice." We know it's sugar.

Five Annoying Things About Being a Waitress at a Trendy Restaurant

—by J. F.

1. When customers on special diets demand that you remove the key ingredient from the chef's specialty.

2. When you're on your way to table 12 and table 10 asks for their bread, not grasping that the kitchen is not between tables 10 and 12, so that it is simply impossible for you, on your return trip past table 10, to miraculously appear with a basket of bread and rosemary-infused olive oil.

PROFESSIONALLY ANNOYED

3. Picky eaters who demand to know every ingredient in every dish on the menu and then say, "I guess I'll just have the penne with tomato sauce."

4. When, at the end of your eight-hour, on-your-feet shift, you're dying to go home, but there's just one table that absolutely refuses to ask for the check, and all you can think about is your ninety-minute commute while they sit there chatting away.

5. When a very large party has just finished their meal and you've entered their bill, only to have them announce, "I'm sorry, but those two over there want a separate bill, I want all my food on my own Amex, those five each want to pay independently, and can we please pay for all the alcohol in cash?"

728. That the internet has turned into a place where you're supposed to justify your existence.

729. When your husband comes home stinking of gin, rushes past you without a kiss, heads for the bathroom, closes the door, turns the faucets on full blast, and yells out, "You go on to bed, honey. . . . I'm gonna be a while."

730. The cruel life lessons that organized sports impart to kids.

731. Orange juice being sold with "No Pulp," "Some Pulp," and "A Lot of Pulp," when what you really crave is "Between No and Some Pulp."

732. What most telescopes are used for.

733. Hysterically checking the places you've already hysterically checked while searching for your wallet.

734. Meek officemates whom you later learn have been playing for keeps behind the scenes all along.

735. That the sober you is never as much fun as the blacked-out you.

736. The humiliation that comes from the endless stream of cars slowing down to watch a cop give you a ticket.

737. That yellow peppers don't receive the credit they deserve.

738. When everywhere you go someone seems to be doing some pointless, noisy task.

739. That aliens in movies almost always look like humans, when in fact they tend to be much smaller.

740. Never anticipating wealth and never receiving it.

741. When the sound of branches scraping against the side of your house scares you even though you're an adult.

742. Paying a toll to cross a bridge you're going the wrong direction on.

743. Remembering the perfect marriage you thought your parents had when you were a child.

744. Having a strong physical attraction to a cartoon character.

745. That deciding not to decide is a decision.

746. When your supervisor asks you to perform an ethically odious task.

747. Waking up and thinking, *It's Monday. Oh wait . . . ahhhh—it's Sunday. Okay, nope, it* is *Monday.*

748. Friends who make a spectacle of themselves.

749. That usually if your bare legs are hanging from stirrups, nothing pleasant is happening.

750. When a call is disconnected right before you say goodbye, forcing you to have to call back to say goodbye.

751. The huge number of people who have never read Tolstoy, Steinbeck, Hemingway, or Scott Cohen.

752. When asked to name a weakness during your job interview, you reply, "I have a slight gambling problem that sometimes leads to theft."

753. Feeling uncomfortable telling someone that she has food wedged between her teeth yet being unable to avert your gaze from it.

754. Fortune cookies that impart no wisdom (e.g., *You are a bundle of energy, always on the go!*).

755. People who get tense during an ostensibly enjoyable occasion, making it difficult for anyone else to enjoy it.

756. That the angels of cleaning never visit your kitchen.

757. Waking up with a stranger's head resting on your shoulder.

758. Realizing that you're completely ignoring the meaning of the words you're reading and wondering how long you've been doing that.

759. That your singing only sounds good when you're alone.

760. People who exaggerate the danger of picking up a piece of broken glass.

761. When you pull your kid's car seat out of your car and find a phantasmagoria of probable-food objects.

762. That bacon will never be considered a vegetable.

763. Being told to go out and find what you need by someone who's already giving you what you need.

764. When an employee walks you over to the product you inquired about and then lingers.

765. That more choice rarely leads to more satisfaction.

766. That there's no way to combine the best aspects of all your prior boyfriends into one super-lovable man.

767. People who feel a need to give you a detailed report of why they're late.

768. When someone mentions at your birthday party that it's her birthday next week too, and it turns into a dual celebration.

769. When a sign says that your car will be towed at the owner's expense, as if you expected someone to appear and say, "Know what? This one's on me."

770. When your complaints about a child could just as easily be applied to you (e.g., "She's going through a phase where everything she wants, she wants it now.").

771. Trying to parent toddlers from the shower.

772. Feeling like an idiot when you realize how common the word is that you couldn't think of (e.g., "A *farm*, of course!").

773. That wrong relationships are more exciting than right ones.

774. When the growing possibility of a simultaneous orgasm ruins that possibility.

775. That I can annoy you. Think not? Noy.

Noy. Noy. Noy. Noy. Noy. Noy. Noy. Noy. Noy. Noy.

NoyNoyNoyNoyNoyNoy.
NoyNoyNoyNoyNoyNoy.
NoyNoyNoyNoyNoyNoy.
NoyNoyNoyNoyNoyNoy.
NoyNoyNoyNoyNoyNoy.

NoyNoyNoyNoyNoyNoy.
NoyNoyNoyNoyNoyNoy.
NoyNoyNoyNoyNoyNoy.
NoyNoyNoyNoyNoyNoy.
NoyNoyNoyNoyNoyNoy.
NoyNoyNoyNoyNoyNoy.
NoyNoyNoyNoyNoyNoy.
NoyNoyNoyNoyNoyNoy.
NoyNoyNoyNoyNoyNoy.
NoyNoyNoyNoyNoyNoy.
NoyNoyNoyNoyNoyNoy.
NoyNoyNoyNoyNoyNoy.
NoyNoyNoyNoyNoyNoy.
NoyNoyNoyNoyNoyNoy.
NoyNoyNoyNoyNoyNoy.
NoyNoyNoyNoyNoyNoy.

| **Don't you just hate that?**

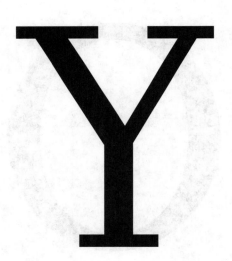

| **Don't you just hate that?**

776. That there's no movie called *Room for Milk*, in which a perky woman in her late thirties juggles aspirations of building a coffee-chain empire with her desire to have kids.

777. When it takes ten years to accept what you knew within minutes.

778. When you feel like you're in a fight with everyone you know.

779. When science fiction dialogue amounts to, "We can't possibly evade the Thepa 480 Starship without fully operational Bloog blasters!"

780. When you order stamps online and the post office charges you shipping.

781. A closed-mouth, nostril-burning soda burp.

782. When you're taking out the garbage and you notice that none of your neighbors have taken their garbage out, making you wonder what day it is.

783. When you're not giving up and they're not giving in.

784. When it takes a procrastinator a long time to admit what he is.

785. That pretending not to see is a crucial parenting technique.

786. When a man you don't know rides your donkey lawn ornament.

787. Unable-to-get-out-of-the-way-of-the-loud-ambulance-behind-me-due-to-the-traffic-in-front-of-me tension.

788. Alcoholic workaholics.

789. When no one can recognize you at your high school reunion.

790. When you start receiving targeted advertisements about planning your own funeral.

791. That convenience stores at night are inherently frightening.

792. Wildly uneven cheese distribution in an omelet.

793. Hoping for an enthusiastic response and getting a noncommittal one.

794. When you bring a salad from the local deli back to work and they forgot to give you a plastic fork.

795. Being told, "*My* money's in the *bank*, sonny!"

796. That the most effective way to tell people to reduce their use of social media is through social media.

797. When your car is stranded on an icy road and the only human within two hundred miles is a Cro-Magnon man wearing a torn parka who communicates through a series of bizarre grunts and gesticulations.

Five Annoying Things About Being a Female Bartender

—by T. W.

1. That countless guys try to be witty by pointing to the bottle opener in my waistband and saying, "Some can openers have all the luck."

2. Foreign tourists who think that nodding their heads is a tip.

3. Groups who order one drink at a time. I don't have time to stand there while you say, "Gin and tonic . . . Hey, Jenny, what do you want? Well, I'm having a gin and tonic. . . . No, it's beer before liquor. . . . Hey, Tommy, what do you guys want?"

4. People who ask for moronic shots like Scooby Snacks, Flaming Lamborghinis, Oatmeal Cookies, Drunken Irish Sailor, Teetering on a Peg Leg with an Italian Grandma (or whatever).

5. People who think they're tough because they order drinks like Thug Passion.

798. When the barber pushes your head around while cutting your hair.

799. When the speaker begins the seminar by saying, "By a show of hands, how many of you don't know the difference between a stock and a bond?" and you're the only one with your hand in the air.

800. Watching the same three bags cycle through the baggage claim area.

801. When you misspell a word so egregiously that Microsoft Word is just like "whatever."

802. That murder is the quickest path to fame.

803. Lifting, then lowering, then lifting your umbrella to avoid colliding with the other umbrellas—none of which seem to ever move up or down.

804. Wondering to what extent a bad habit of yours has become a vice.

805. That at some point in the future, $2,000 will buy you a pack of gum.

806. Personalized license plates that tell you the driver's occupation (e.g., CPA PAUL).

807. Wanting to express your feelings to the person you like but fearing you'll scare them away.

808. Those inane comedy and tragedy masks that represent the theater.

809. When seeing a homeless woman sleeping on a park bench stirs less compassion in you than watching an old dog limp along.

810. That *Saturday Night Fever* was a good movie— perhaps a great one—but it unleashed some very ugly forces, particularly in Brooklyn and Staten Island.

811. When wearing a bib while eating lobster in a restaurant makes you feel like an adult baby.

812. Helping a friend move back into your living room.

813. Wondering *Now what?* after your favorite team has just won the Super Bowl.

814. Reading a sign, three hours into your hike, that says, IN THE EVENT THAT A BLACK BEAR ATTACKS, USE EVERYTHING AVAILABLE—INCLUDING YOUR HANDS—TO FIGHT BACK!

815. Feeling bad about what you didn't say.

816. When the piñata at your five-year-old son's birthday party proves unbreakable.

817. Meeting your teacher's husband at the end-of-the-year picnic and realizing that she is not an unhinged tyrant, but a real person with a family that loves and depends on her.

818. When someone enters the elevator and sees that you've already pushed "Lobby," but pushes it anyway.

819. That there's no point to signing the back of your credit card.

820. Driving to a bar, getting rip-roaring drunk, doing the responsible thing and getting a ride home, and waking up the next morning with no idea where you parked your car the night before.

821. The amount of control complete strangers wield over your life.

822. When a slight change in your date's expression makes you realize you'll be going home alone.

823. Bending to pick up the subscription cards that fell out of the magazine you're reading.

824. Finding your brother-in-law alone in the living room on all fours pretending lord-knows-what.

825. How hard it has become to use a TV.

826. A passenger safety pamphlet in an airplane depicting a smiling woman strapping a flotation vest around a little girl's neck.

827. The obligatory twenty-minute drum solo at any jam-band outdoor concert.

828. When you say, "God bless you," to the person who sneezed and he replies, "It was a cough."

829. The fact that you were supposed to flip your mattress over nine years ago.

830. Listening to someone clip their nails on a train.

831. The percentage of crab in most crab cakes.

832. Do you want me to lower the air conditioner? Is the music too loud? Should I open a window? Here—you don't drink enough water.

833. Carefully unfolding each corner of a beat-up dollar before inserting it into a vending machine, only to have it come back again. And again.

834. When the trauma of being broken up with causes your ex to lose weight and look great.

835. When someone puts their two-year-old on the phone and you're like, *What am I supposed to say to this person—should I start mooing?*

836. "As always, your privacy is your right and our privilege." I HAVE NO PRIVACY, YOU AUTOMATED ROBOT-SCHMUCK.

837. When the agony of turning fifty makes you regret how depressed you felt on your fortieth birthday.

838. People who are so smart they're stupid.

839. When the person you're ready to hook up with keeps drinking.

840. When the gas company tells you that they won't charge you for a visit "unless the problem is on your end."

841. People who attach deep significance to their moronic tattoos (e.g., "The fire-breathing gargoyles on my shoulder represent my disdain for organized religion.").

842. Any form of entertainment that features imprisoned animals.

843. People who hold a door open for you when you're sort of far away, causing you to walk faster.

844. The strain of maintaining that Grandma is an endlessly benevolent person and not the manipulative bully you know her to be.

845. That pancakes aren't considered a dessert.

846. Having no idea what the digital billboard with a constantly increasing sixteen-digit number stands for.

847. The sound of acrylic fingernails tap-tap-tapping a countertop.

848. Knowing that you succeeded by identifying and exploiting other people's weaknesses.

849. Not being able to name one event that occurred between 967 and 1492.

850. When movie characters wake up and make out with each other without brushing their teeth.

851. Being part of an angry crowd.

852. When you're trying on clothes and a salesperson knocks on the door and asks if everything's all right in there.

853. When you want to socialize with the other dogs and your owner won't let you.

854. The anxious inner dialogue you experience prior to introducing yourself to a large group.

855. That the most intense laughter usually comes at the least appropriate time.

856. When the fortune-teller tells your wife, "You will have all sorts of adventures with all sorts of men."

857. Knowing that an acquaintance is going through a disturbing life experience and that she knows you know, as you continue making small talk.

858. When a young child receives a gift he already has, and he says, "I already have this."

859. When someone tells you, "I'm surrounded by insane people," and you're the only other person in the room.

860. Knowing that your popcorn crunching is annoying other people in the movie theater.

861. Peoplewhotalkfastlikethis.

862. Guests who use your shower and don't towel-dry themselves, drenching the little rug.

863. That a thirty-minute rubbernecking delay is just as likely to be caused by a minor fender bender as by a serious accident in which there's really something worth slowing down to see.

864. That you wouldn't have the faintest idea if your accountant was ripping you off.

865. Losing the only jacket that ever made you feel cool.

866. The petty bickering that goes on at your synagogue.

867. Nodding off during your drug trial.

Five Annoying Things About Being a Copy Editor

—by S. T.

1. That the 487,206th time you look up the word "makeup," it *still* doesn't have a hyphen.

2. That you can spend two months of your life absorbing every tiny scrap of information about raising chickens, and have no memory of the subject a week later.

3. When the author insists that his way is the correct way to spell something, and after protracted arguments you find out he's right.

4. That nobody knows the rules of use of commas with restrictive versus nonrestrictive appositive clauses.

5. When you find a Post-it on the floor that says, *Absolutely MUST confirm this*, with an arrow pointing to something on the page to which the Post-it was formerly stuck.

868. The near impossibility of leaving a buffet without feeling bloated.

869. Bridges with ridges that make you wonder if you have a flat tire that's dire.

870. When the people picked to fix the crisis are the ones who created it.

871. When lemonade contains artificial flavors, and dishwashing fluid is made with real lemons.

872. Hiding your lack of emotional generosity by giving gifts.

873. When the groom's poem for the bride rhymes "soul mate" with "jailbait."

874. Watching the era you grew up in go from the recent past to retro to ancient history.

875. That even the healthy nut crunch cereals are loaded with sugar.

876. That you can never remember someone's name after they've been introduced to you.

877. Wondering if you are behaving immorally by continuing to enjoy the emotional connection you have with another married person.

878. That if higher forms of life have been observing humankind, they've shown little willingness to help us avert the apocalypse.

879. Gone are the days when sleeping in a "big boy bed" filled your nights with wonder.

880. That humans have about 60,000 thoughts per day, 59,053 of which they've thought previously.

881. Not knowing whether to ask a dog owner: "Can I pet him?" or "Can I pet her?" or "Can I pet it?"

882. Wildly unhealthy coffee orders ("Yeah, give me a Venti double mocha with a triple shot of espresso, five Splendas, and two creams.").

883. Documentary reenactments that use close-ups (e.g., plump fingers wrapped around a whiskey bottle in an Elvis biography).

884. Leaving the only house that ever made you happy.

885. When hot dog sales at a ballgame exceed attendance.

886. People who give status reports about their overall level of physical comfort (e.g., "My ears are cold, and my feet are a bit dry.").

887. When all your heavy groceries are loaded into one bag and all the light groceries into the other.

888. When a stranger comes up to you and says, "Terry?"

889. When a good friend moves ten minutes away from you, and you still barely see her.

890. When someone's advice is to ignore all advice.

891. Pre-recorded, lip-synched national anthems.

892. When a highlighter veers into the wrong line.

893. EdwardSchnerb @EdwardSchnerb.com.

894. When eating a stack of hot-out-of-the-oven chocolate chip cookies becomes more of an athletic event than a culinary experience.

895. That the amount of money gambled on the Super Bowl could wipe out entire social problems.

896. Holding a grudge toward an inanimate object.

897. When biceps are referred to as "guns."

898. When an online work meeting turns into basically a bunch of people saying, "No, you go ahead."

899. Accidentally chewing tinfoil.

900. Waiting to be handed a receipt that you will immediately scrunch into a ball and toss out.

901. That your heart rate increases whenever you hear the word "casino."

902. When lies, deceit, and manipulation cause you to eat a tub of ice cream.

903. When the worst part of someone's golf game is their personality.

904. Confronting a naked liar.

905. Never knowing whether to call it "seltzer," "club soda," or "sparkling water."

906. Questionably recyclable objects.

907. When_a_file_
name_has_these_idiot_
underlines_between_each_
word.

908. That if a corporation
will boost profits by
wasting your time . . .
they'll waste your time.

909. Anyone who tells
you, "You work with a lion
the same way you would a
human."

910. A stampede of eighth-graders.

911. That attractive people receive more "God bless you"s.

912. When you first learn that there is no Santa Claus and realize it's only one of the many lies you've been told.

913. Only remembering why you walked into the other room when you return to the one you came from.

914. That hot dogs usually come in packages of ten and rolls come in packages of eight.

915. That "down for" and "up for" mean the same thing.

916. That the ride there always seems longer than the ride home.

917. When someone who can't make a decision decides to flip a coin and then considers flipping again.

918. When your phone is at 10 percent battery life but it suddenly dies.

919. Peeled sticker residue on an apple.

920. When your dentist talks to you while he's working on your teeth and your only contributions to the conversation are "eshk" and "zguhshzsck."

921. Strangers who think they have the right to rub your belly because you're pregnant.

922. When a conversation is the equivalent of the other person repeatedly smacking a tennis ball out of bounds, and then you sprinting and managing to return the ball.

923. The large number of factors, most of which are beyond your control, that determine whether you have fun at a party.

924. Never knowing where to put those extra buttons that come with fancy shirts.

925. When someone who is arrested for robbing vending machines pays their bail in quarters.

926. When you tell a child, "Oh, enough with the fake crying!" and the crying becomes real.

927. When your opponent has you in a mounted crucifix and he's already broken your nose, leg, and orbital.

928. When you stare at your face in a mirror and enter a hazy netherworld of mild dissatisfaction.

929. Paying money to lose money. Doesn't happen? You'll learn.

930. When there are no good movies out in theaters for months and then there are five films you want to see.

931. When the quotation marks in an email are transformed into symbols (e.g., So I say to my family, ℧%* What is this, some kind of an intervention? Ω☺⊠ ™).

932. When a video of someone "baby birding" chewed food into their friend's mouth gets 17 million views.

933. The natural aptitude kids have for scratching surfaces.

934. When your waiter keeps saying "I have" while reading the specials.

935. Fearing you're nearing the wall while swimming the backstroke in a pool.

936. When you break up with someone and their reaction makes you wonder why you didn't do it sooner.

937. When a goat falls through your ceiling.

938. When everything around and in you feels profoundly sad, which validates your suspicion that there's something wrong with you, which saddens you further, which convinces you that it will always be like this, it will never be different, when in fact you will eventually find wonder, purpose, and sustained contentment.

939. Trying to conduct a serious conversation with the hiccups.

940. When a cop flashes his lights and siren at you and the only available space on the side of the road is in front of a fire hydrant.

941. When a children's toy, unprompted, starts laughing maniacally.

942. When Sunday feels like an interminable wait for Monday.

943. When the line for the women's bathroom is ten times longer than the men's.

944. When the car behind you is moving, but you can't see anyone in it.